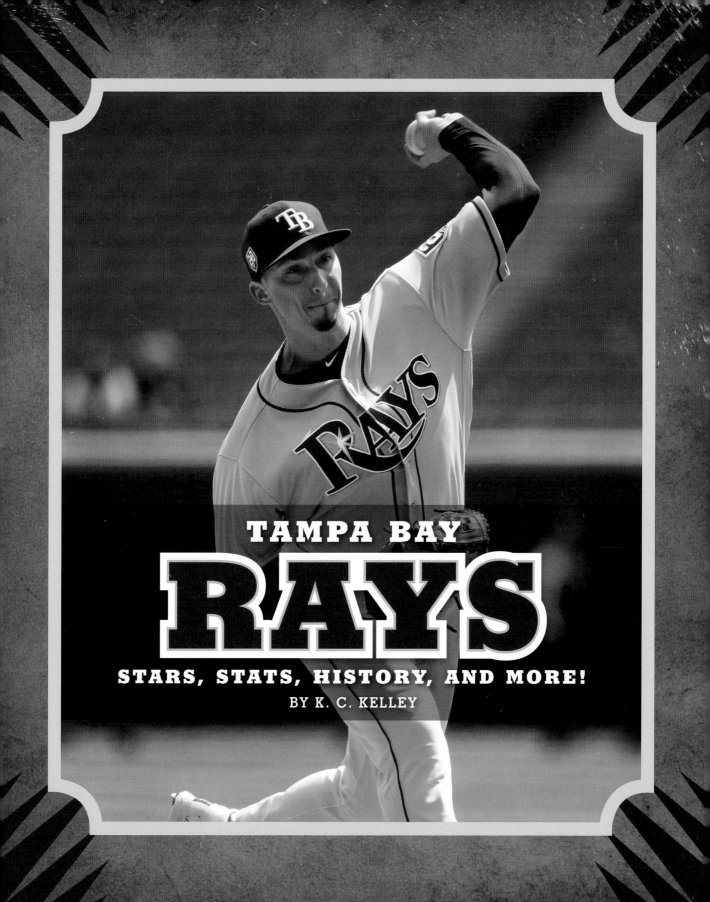

TAMPA BAY
RAYS

STARS, STATS, HISTORY, AND MORE!

BY K. C. KELLEY

Published by The Child's World®
1980 Lookout Drive • Mankato, MN 56003-1705
800-599-READ • www.childsworld.com

ISBN 9781503828407
LCCN 2018944855

Printed in the United States of America
PAO2392

Photo Credits:
Cover: Joe Robbins (2).
Interior: AP Images: Steve Nesins 9, Ted S. Warren 19,
Chris O'Meara 20; Dreamstime.com: Patrick Goodwin
13; Newscom: Rhona Wise/Icon SMI 17; Joe Robbins:
5, 6, 10, 23, 24, 27, 29; Shutterstock: Eric Broder van
Dyke 14;

About the Author

K.C. Kelley is a huge sports
fan who has written more
than 100 books for kids. His
favorite sport is baseball.
He has also written about
football, basketball, soccer,
and even auto racing! He lives
in Santa Barbara, California.

On the Cover

Main photo: Pitcher Blake Snell
Inset: Former Tampa Bay star
James Shields

CONTENTS

GO, RAYS!

The Tampa Bay Rays are one of baseball's newest teams. They thrilled their fans in Florida with a spot in the 2008 World Series. They are still looking to earn another spot in the championship series. The Rays might be in a new ballpark soon. Will that bring them good luck? Let's meet the Rays!

Speedy Mallex Smith is part of a great group of young Rays players. ➤

WHO ARE THE RAYS?

The Rays play in the American League (AL). That group is part of Major League Baseball (MLB). MLB also includes the National League (NL). There are 30 teams in MLB. The winner of the AL plays the winner of the NL in the **World Series**. The Rays have not won a World Series yet. Their fans hope that day will come soon!

◄ *Matt Duffy is a key infielder for the Rays.*

WHERE THEY CAME FROM

The Rays joined MLB in 1998. They were added to the AL. Tampa Bay became the first MLB team in Florida! At first, the Tampa Bay team was called the Devil Rays. That's the name of a sea creature that lives near Florida. In 2008, the team dropped the "Devil" part. It must have helped. That was the year the Rays made the World Series!

Pitcher Dennis Springer wears the original ➤
Devil Rays uniform in 1998.

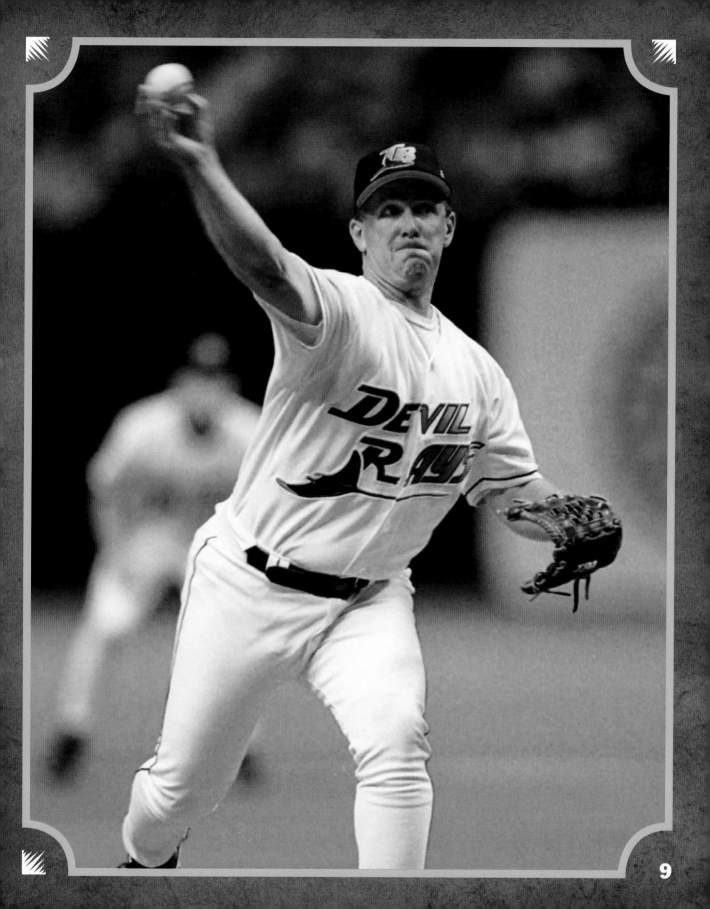

WHO THEY PLAY

The Rays play in the AL East Division. The other teams in the AL East are the Baltimore Orioles, the Boston Red Sox, the New York Yankees, and the Toronto Blue Jays. The Rays play more games against their division **rivals** than against other teams. In all, Tampa Bay plays 162 games each season. The Rays play 81 games at home and 81 on the road.

◄ *First baseman C.J. Cron will play a big part in Tampa Bay's future.*

WHERE THEY PLAY

The Rays have played in Tropicana Field since their first season. The ballpark is indoors. The players play under a huge sloping roof. The field has **artificial turf**, not real grass. The Rays have said they are building a new ballpark that will have a see-through roof!

Fans hope to move out of Tropicana Field and into a new ballpark. ➤

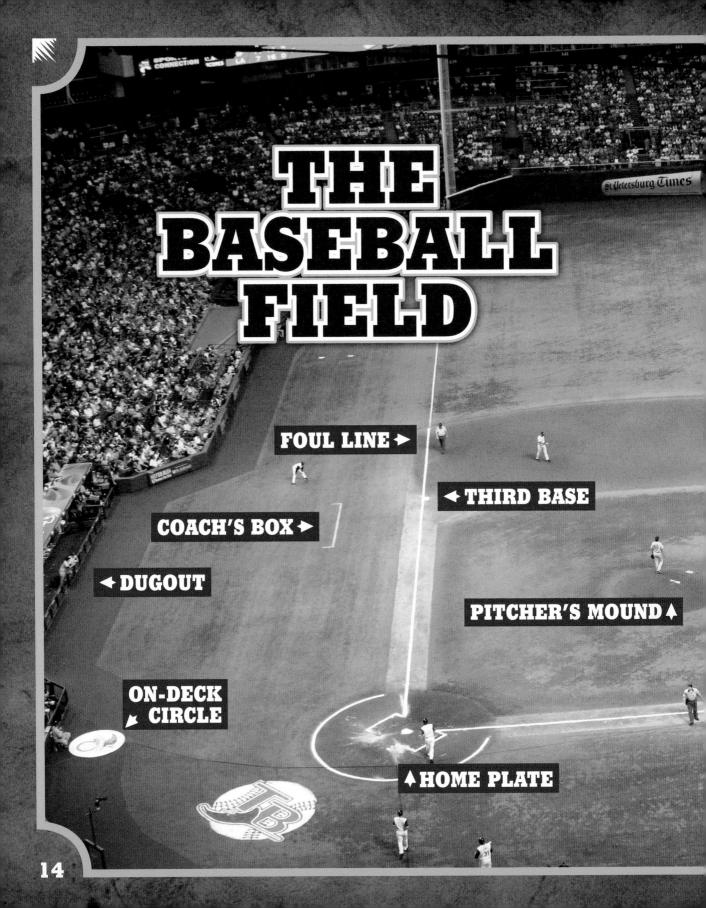

THE BASEBALL FIELD

FOUL LINE ➤

◄ THIRD BASE

COACH'S BOX ➤

PITCHER'S MOUND ▲

◄ DUGOUT

ON-DECK
CIRCLE ▼

▲ HOME PLATE

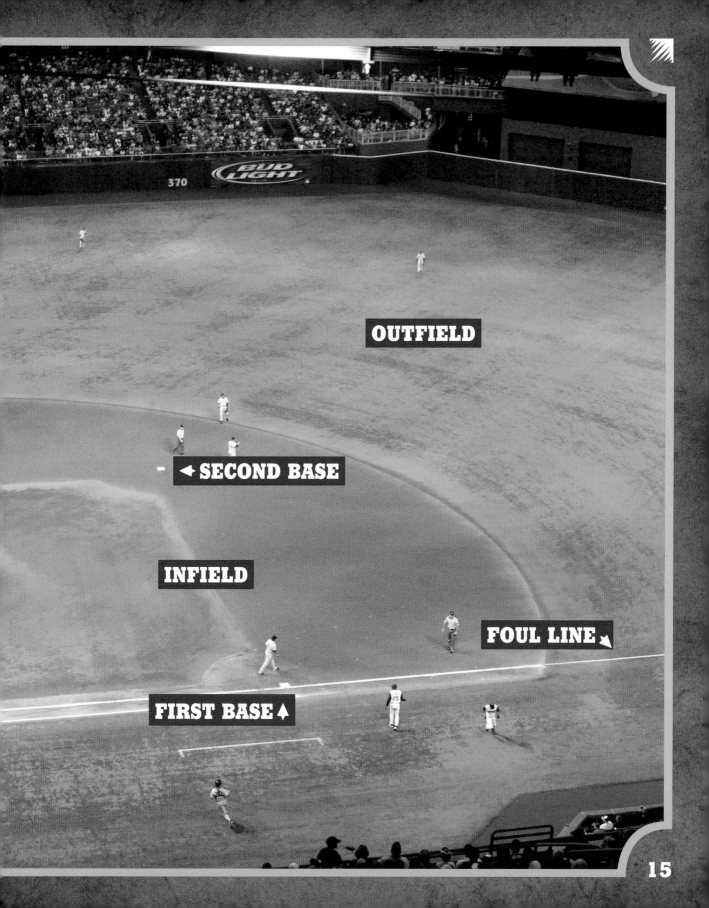

OUTFIELD

◄ SECOND BASE

INFIELD

FOUL LINE ◣

FIRST BASE ▲

BIG DAYS

The Rays have had some great days in their short history. Here are a few of them.

1999—Hall of Famer Wade Boggs joined the Rays. He thrilled fans by getting his 3,000th career hit on August 7. It was a home run!

2008—The Rays won their first AL **pennant**. It sent them to their only World Series (so far!).

2010—Matt Garza threw the only **no-hitter** in Rays history. He beat the Detroit Tigers and did not allow a hit!

Dogpile! The Rays jump for joy after winning ➤
the American League in 2008.

TOUGH DAYS

Like every team, the Rays have had some not-so-great days, too. Here are a few their fans might not want to recall.

2002—The Rays have had more losing seasons than winning seasons. Their worst was 2002. The team lost 106 games!

2012—Seattle's Felix Hernandez threw a **perfect game** against the Rays. It was the third time Tampa Bay had given one up. That's the most perfect games any team has given up of all time.

2016—Talk about bad streaks! The Rays lost 24 out of 27 games at one point this season.

During a 2012 game, "King Felix" Hernandez ➤ *didn't allow a single baserunner to the Rays.*

MEET THE FANS!

Tampa Bay has some very wet "fans." A huge touch tank at Tropicana Field is home to rays. Fans can visit these sea animals before home games. Six players have hit home runs that landed in the rays' tank! The team has three **mascots**. Raymond Ray and Stinger are rays. DJ Kitty gets fans dancing with great music.

← *Two rays are about to be put into the giant water tank at Tropicana Field.*

HEROES THEN

The best player in Rays history now plays for the San Francisco Giants. Third baseman Evan Longoria played for the Rays from 2008–2017. He holds most of the team's batting records. Carl Crawford was another Rays star. He combined power with great speed on the bases. Pitchers Matt Garza and James Shields helped the Rays win the 2008 AL pennant.

Evan Longoria was a great hitter for the Rays for 10 seasons. ➤

HEROES NOW

Tampa Bay's 2018 All-Star was starting pitcher Blake Snell. He was among the best pitchers in the AL all season. **Designated hitter** C.J. Cron slugged a lot of homers. Kevin Kiermaier is a great outfielder on defense. Closer Sergio Romo has an awesome slider. That's a pitch that looks like a fastball to the hitter. Then the pitch curves as it comes near the plate.

◄ *Blake Snell has become one of the AL's top left-handed pitchers.*

GEARING UP

Baseball players wear team uniforms. On defense, they wear leather gloves to catch the ball. As batters, they wear hard helmets. This protects them from pitches. Batters hit the ball with long wood bats. Each player chooses his own size of bat. Catchers have the toughest job. They wear a lot of protection.

THE BASEBALL

The outside of the Major League baseball is made from cow leather. Two leather pieces shaped like 8s are stitched together. There are 108 stitches of red thread. These stitches help players grip the ball. Inside, the ball has a small center of cork and rubber. Hundreds of feet of yarn are tightly wound around this center.

CATCHER'S HELMET

WRIST BANDS

CATCHER'S MITT

CHEST PROTECTOR

SHIN GUARDS

CATCHER'S GEAR

TEAM STATS

ere are some of the all-time career records for the Tampa Bay Rays. All of these stats are through the 2018 regular season.

HOME RUNS	
Evan Longoria	261
Carlos Pena	163

RBI	
Evan Longoria	892
Carl Crawford	592

BATTING AVERAGE	
Carl Crawford	.296
James Loney	.291

STOLEN BASES	
Carl Crawford	409
Melvin Upton Jr.	232

WINS	
James Shields	87
David Price	82

SAVES	
Roberto Hernandez	101
Alex Colome	95

James Shields played for the Rays for the first seven seasons of his career. ➤

STRIKEOUTS

James Shields	1,250
Chris Archer	1,146

GLOSSARY

artificial turf (ar-tih-FISH-ul TURF) ground cover made from plastic that looks like real grass

designated hitter (DEZ-ig-NAY-tid HIT-ter) known as the DH, a position in the AL that replaces the pitcher in the batting order

mascots (MASS-cot) costumed characters who help fans cheer

no-hitter (no-HIT-er) a game in which the starting pitcher wins and does not allow a hit to the opponent

pennant (PEN-ent) a triangular piece of cloth that symbolizes winning a league championship

perfect game (PER-fekt GAYM) a game in which the starting pitcher wins and does not allow a single baserunner

rivals (RYE-vuhlz) two people or groups competing for the same thing

World Series (WURLD SEE-reez) the annual championship of Major League Baseball

FIND OUT MORE

IN THE LIBRARY

Connery-Boyd, Peg. *Tampa Bay Rays: The Big Book of Activities*. Chicago, IL: Sourcebooks, Jabberwocky, 2016.

Jacobs, Greg. *The Everything Kids' Baseball Book: 10th Edition*. New York, NY: Adams Media, 2016.

Sports Illustrated Kids (editors). *The Big Book of Who: Baseball*. New York, NY: Sports Illustrated Kids, 2017.

ON THE WEB

Visit our website for links about the Tampa Bay Rays: **childsworld.com/links**

Note to Parents, Teachers, and Librarians: We routinely verify our web links to make sure they are safe and active sites. So encourage your readers to check them out!

INDEX